BLOOM in Word

A Poetic Journey of Finding Purpose in Pain

Published by Erika Brown

Paperback ISBN: 979-8-9879879-3-3
eBook ISBN: 979-8-9879879-8-8

Cover Design: Erika Brown
Cover Photo Credit: Couleur from Pexels
Interior Design: Erika Brown
Edited By: Valerie Dial

A Poetic Journey of Finding Purpose in Pain

Erika Brown

Contents

Section Three: Unravel

Section Four: Lotus Flower

Section Five: Blossom

I dedicate this book to every teardrop, every doubt, every insecurity, every storm, every heartbreak, and every time I questioned my "enoughness."

I would not be who I am or where I am without it

My intention for this book is to let 'her' know she is not alone

and

to encourage anyone in the midst of the storm to hold on...

Bloom inWord Playlist

As a lover of both music and words, I created a playlist for you to listen to as you read. Scan the QR code at the bottom of the page to access the playlist.

Shackles - Mary Mary
Stomp (Remix) - Kirk Franklin's Nu Nation
Under the Influence - Anointed
The Storm Is Over Now - Kirk Franklin's Nu Nation
You'll Always Be My Baby - Mariah Carey
Tha Crossroads - Bone Thugs - N - Harmony
Open My Heart - Yolanda Adams
Numb/Encore - Jay Z & Linkin Park
Back That Azz Up - Juvenile, Mannie Fresh & Lil Wayne
Killing Me Softly With His Song - Fugees & Ms. Lauryn Hill
Toma - Pitbull & Lil Jon
Standing Ovation - Young Jeezy
Bang - Young Jeezy feat. T.I. & Lil Scrappy
Knuck If You Buck - Crime Mob & Lil Scrappy
Warrior - Yo Gotti
Closer - Goapele
Dance Tonight - Lucy Pearl
Bad - Wale feat. Tiara Thomas
Suffocate - J Holiday
Drop the World - Eminem & Lil Wayne
The Best In Me - Marvin Sapp
Take Care - Drake & Rihanna
Take Me To the King - Tamela Mann
Good Mourning - India.Aire
Blame It On Me - Chrisette Michele
Is There Somewhere - Halsey
Peace Sign - Rick Ross
Hearts Ain't Gonna Lie - Arlissa
Fly Before You Fall - Cynthia Erivo
Ready For Love - India.Aire
All the Way - Ledisi

Welcome

I look into my daughter's eyes and without hesitation, a smile eases across my face. I often wonder and ask myself how did I get here. The answer is neither far nor hard to decipher as it stares back at me every time I gaze in the mirror. I wonder what's next and I tremble with fear at the thought of me sabotaging something else. Me getting in the way of me and my greatness.

But last night before I drifted away into peace and quiet I wrote, 'Experience'. And 'Experience' gave me the clarity that regardless of the outcome of the experience, the gift was the experience. I told my Mom today that experiences begin and end but I realize now life is never-ending. In life, I have choices and options and it is up to me as to whether or not I allow my experiences to make or break me because see, experiences are going to continue to happen.

I no longer want to tremble with fear as I prepare for my future. I often get frustrated and discouraged at the idea of plans, dreams, and hopes as so many of those plans, dreams, and hopes failed to become my reality. Again, there are no fingers to point or people to blame as I am the one it all started and ended with. Like a movie or TV show, people played their roles but I believe in the analogy that people are placed in our lives for a reason and a season.

I like to give credit where credit is due and as much as I've done in a place of self-will...God, my creator, is truly the Author of this narrative I've entitled, 'Life'. Because of the being God is, he need not force himself, he gave me the gift of free will. However, regardless of my stunts, tricks, and/or antics, he promised never to leave nor forsake me and he loves me enough to allow me to dive into my experiences head first with a towel on deck as I pencil in that last period. So this here is a testimony, my story of where I've been and where I am. One of the biggest lessons I've learned through it all is to engulf myself fully in the moment.

Experiences come and go and although some may be similar...no two are exactly alike. So regardless of the smiles, tears, excitement, pain, and so on and so forth...if I am not present in the here and now I miss out on the totality of the experience. And each experience is truly a gift. This here journey you're about to embark upon with me is filled with twists, turns, ups, and downs, so please buckle your seatbelt and enjoy the ride through the makings of me...

Section One:

Daddy Issues

Once Upon A Time

A look of desire
A compliment to the way I switch my hips
The dip in my back, the shiver down my spine
A melodic description of the goings on between the sheets
The way you lick your lips has me fantasizing about your southern skill set
Tickets to your show sold out by your wordplay
Aspirations of being your girl has me down for whatever, ready to prove to you how worthy I am for a night of your attention that in my core I long to last forever
Baited by your charm and hooked by your generic compliments needing so badly to be seen
Going above and beyond required measures in desperation of possibly being chosen
Chose not because of the light that burns within but because of the attention I bring as I adorn your arm
As the magnifying glass brings the hazy image closer, there is a small child with her head hanging low, lost, looking for solace in anyone or anything that will temporarily fill these gnawing gaps and holes within her
But when the magnifying glass is put up and the naked eye rests upon me again, I resort back to statistical status...

Rose

Piece by piece my heart breaks...like a flower that loses its petals...I slowly lose the idea of us.
Caught in a whirlwind of feelings and emotions I was swept off my feet at the idea of us.
My dream come true was only a borrowed, undiscovered treasure that belonged to someone else.
Like a newly released book from the library, I had to return you.
In reading the pages I became lost in a fantasy world filled with I Dos and Happily Ever After...but as I turned the last page there was no more...the story of us was over.

I Thought

I thought the unerasable thoughts of you were signs I wasn't moving forward
I thought the overwhelming feelings of sadness, hurt, confusion, and anger were signs I was unable to shake you
I thought the uncontrollable flashbacks of stills of us were signs I wanted those times back
I thought the tears that flowed day after day were a sign I was still lost in you
I thought I was stuck at a standstill but I see now these were all actually signs of healing
I've never taken the time to sit and feel
Feelings overwhelm me and they scare me
But this is a lesson worth learning so I don't have to come back here again
So all that I'm going through and all that is happening is actually just the process of cleansing and growth
I'm not running anymore and I'm not hiding anymore
I thought you scarred me but really you unveiled me...

Perfect

What we had was perfect, right?
What we had started on a lie, so it could never be perfect...
Swept off my feet and carried away to faraway places like Neverland and Once Upon a Time...
Blinded by infatuation although I could have sworn it was love
Faded as the words, "Hi, I'm __________, how are you..." forever changed my life
Gazing out of the window daydreaming of "him" when out of the blue you bent the corner and walked into my life
I thought you were my gift from God, my other half, my happily ever after
But what started on a lie, could never be perfect...
I bought every dream you ever put up for sale...I emptied my pockets investing in what I thought was forever
Captivated by your wordplay I was oblivious to your actions connecting the dots to my impending fall back down to the slums of reality from my newly built mansion on cloud nine
Stepping out on a limb to follow my heart and trust our connection...the branch was weak, I fell, and you stood back and watched my fall
You told me you had me and I believed you
You made me feel safe, desired, and understood
You looked into my eyes and I felt you inside of me
You touched me with a purpose that electrified my soul
You were what I dreamt of when I had the opportunity to piece together the perfect "him"
But what started as a lie, could never be perfect
Peeling back the layers, my true colors are discovered
As the chair slowly turns to reveal the one responsible for my pain...it is me I see... guilty as charged
How could this be, when it is you who clearly did all of this to me?
Because it is I who made a choice in a split second to pursue the unattainable and overlook what was clearly right in front of me...

Wrong & Right

I've heard of love at first sight but this was something deeper. I thanked God for him and seconds later he appeared. I was at a loss for words as this gift was bestowed upon me. When I met him face to face, I looked into his eyes and was re-introduced to his soul. As our hands touched my heart literally skipped a beat. His smile sent a tingle down my spine and his energy was warm and unforgettable. After his departure, I was left in a tizzy as God's gift to me was already unwrapped by another. As the days and weeks passed I tried to erase his smile, his gaze, his touch, and his very presence from my memory. When our paths intertwined I attempted to keep our interactions short, sweet, and to the point. I was raised in the church and freshly divorced knowing all too well about women who ignored the all too visible ring that adorned the left hand. With my head, I went into every interaction with him with my compass of right and wrong fully calibrated. But on 'Day One' the door of my heart opened and instead of shutting it per my head's request, I left it cracked for "what if" to step in...

Everything Happens For A Reason

Self-examination to find the cause
The cause of my pain...
What did I do?
What didn't I do?
What should I have done?
What could I have done?
Day by day...
Piece by piece...
Little by little...
More of my heart breaks...
Interrogation of myself,
    the crime?
        Losing you...
Everything Happens For A Reason
Memories of you...
    Your laugh
    Your smile
    Your "quotes"
    The look in your eyes...
    Your personality
    Your uniqueness
Memories of us...
    Laid up
    Playing
    Cuddling
    Late night chats
    The way you held me
    The connection
All the good times
All the bad times
Like a song on repeat
Steadily replaying in my mind

Everything Happens For A Reason
Tears visit me nightly
New emotions, never felt before
Indescribable pain, not physical but emotional
Thinking unclear, blocked by thoughts of you
Mind games…
   Are you okay?
   What are you doing?
   Are you thinking about me?
   Do you miss me?
   Have you found my replacement?
   Why won't you fight for me?
Everything Happens For A Reason
Were you just in my life for a season,
to show me what it's like to love?
I feel like we could have been together forever…
The way we click,
like we were just meant to be
You opened my eyes to a whole new world…
A world full of happiness, acceptance, realness, and joy
But in the blink of an eye,
you showed me a different world…
A world full of
   misunderstanding,
   pain,
   and confusion
They say when love is good…it's really good
And when it's bad…it's really bad
But at the end of the day,
   if I had to choose
   between loving or not loving at all
I would choose to love, just to do it again with you
Everything Happens For A Reason
The reason…unknown

I Can't Shake You

I blink my eyes in hopes that it will erase the thoughts of you. I take a deep breath in hopes that it will bring me back to reality. I pray and ask God to help me let you go.
I can't shake you...
You're everywhere; I hear your voice, I see your smile, I'm tickled by your laugh, I have to remind myself to inhale and exhale as I embrace the remembrance of your touch, I become lost in the memories of us as I gaze up at the stars once night falls, you sleep with me daily and hold me close as you're in my dreams.
I can't shake you...
I know far too well the difference between right and wrong. I want so badly to do right but the thought of you not in my life cripples me with sadness. I've lived a life without you in it but my exposure to you has left me unwilling to travel back down the road of what once was.
I can't shake you...
Questions with no answers, equations with no solutions, races with no finish lines, stories with no ending, sentences with no periods
I can't shake you...
I saw happily ever after and now I unsuccessfully attempt to wipe my eyes like windshield wipers as the tears cascade down my face as I must accept what is instead of what I wish to be. You opened my eyes to a world I never knew existed. I chased my dreams, followed my heart, and found you.
I can't shake you...
It started with a poem and is now ending with a poem as the story of us has reached its final sentences. I can't shake you and I may never shake you. But I have to turn the last page and return the book of you. You were an amazing, captivating, enthralling, tantalizing, and priceless story that will forever hold a special place in my heart.
I can't shake you...but I'm letting you go.

The Missing Period

I blink my eyes in hopes of getting a better look at the stranger sitting across from me
I tilt my head ever so slightly in hopes of fixing the blurry image I'm trying to capture
I ask myself how we went from lovers to enemies each fighting for a separate cause
The sound of your voice that once upon a time made me melt now is similar to the sound of nails across a chalkboard
The butterflies that used to stir up my stomach have metamorphosed into our unborn child's kicks under the table
A child so pure, so innocent, so beautiful...that if I heard you correctly will be on reserve to meet her Daddy until he receives permission from the Master
Waiting patiently for the Director to say cut so I can exhale and regroup from this emotional scene unfolding before me
I feel my feelings and emotions begin to boil so I reach for the knob to turn down the heat but as I touch it, it disintegrates in my hand
I collect the remnants of what once was, compose myself ever so gracefully, free myself from the confines of you, stand tall on my feet, push my chair in because of course sir, I'm a lady, look at you one last time and walk away from the latest chapter in my book...

Why?

Why do we choose his happiness over our own?
Why do we fight for his attention and words of affirmation instead of fighting for our worth and respect?
Why do we become weak in the knees at the twinkle in his eye, his cool and calm hello, or his repetitive I'm sorry?
Why do we lose sleep waiting for his text or call or to finally feel him crawl into bed?
Why do we patiently wait for him to leave her in hopes he won't do to us what he's done to her?
Why do we allow him to slide in raw knowing we're not the only one he's laying beside?
Why do we believe his empty promises knowing time and time again his actions speak louder than his words?
Why are we willing to lose ourselves in desperation for just a moment with him?
Why do we keep going back praying for something different while all along knowing deep within that he's not ready to change?
Why do we allow a title, a role, or a dollar amount to keep us hostage to heartache, pain, bondage, and misery?
Why do we allow his touch on our favorite spot to put us in a temporary coma?
Why do we see all the signs and red flags yet proceed forward thinking this one or this time will be different?
Why do we give away our power as women to become love-struck puppets?
No for real, why...

Just For Today

Just for today
I'm sad and my heart is weighing heavy
But I don't want you
Just for today
I lay in bed reminiscing on our times together
But I'm not looking to create new memories with you
Just for today
Not only do I ask the question why...
But I too am willing to accept the why not...
Just for today
I see a future without you in it and I'm okay with that
Just for today
I see her and I feel her pain
Just for today
I see you and understand why it's a blessing you chose to leave me
Just for today
I'm grateful for losing you because you made space for "him"
Just for today
I know that this too shall pass but I'm going to find solace in the here and now

You

There's a gap
There's a space
There's a divot
I need you to fill it...
I need you to feel whole...
I need you to extinguish this fire that's ablaze within me when I'm without you
I need you to be my guiding light through the darkness that washes over me when I am alone
Pulling, yearning, ripping...sinking
Help!!
Without you, I feel empty
Without you, happiness escapes me
Without you, I feel naked and exposed for the world to see
But wait...
What is this I see rising above the horizon?
That you I seek is really me...
My insecurity
My fear
My false truths
My past
My never agains
My distorted stills of what life is
Running from me in hopes of finding you as you fill my lungs like a thin layer of smoke that carries me away to not now nor then
You are what I cling to in hopes of not dealing with what is
Tired...
On the verge of excavating the authentic me I cover my eyes and run and hide...

Right Here/Right Now

For a moment in time, I was lost in the translation
The world as I knew it slipped through my fingertips as I unknowingly opened Pandora's Box
I became oblivious to life as I once knew it and became enthralled in all that was you
Your texts started and ended my day
Your voice was my AM cup of coffee
Your touch was intoxicating and I became addicted
I promised myself I wouldn't become entangled
But by the time I felt myself sinking into the quicksand...it was too late...I was stuck
I fought tirelessly to escape the hold you had on me
You broke me into tiny pieces and scattered me across the seven seas and then sat by idly as I scrambled to uncover, discover, and grab hold of the pieces of me
With each piece I found, I looked to you
I looked to you for solace
And in your eyes, I saw nothing
What once held a warm light was now dark and empty
I told myself I could let you go
I told myself I would never chase a man
I told myself I was worthy of more
However, these things I told myself were not depicted in my daily steps through each day, each week, and each month...I clung to you like a relentless piece of lint on a cashmere sweater
I prayed, I cried, I journaled, I swore, I read, I begged...and time and time again I was unable to shake you
So today I embrace the here and now as I try this thing called acceptance
No longer will I fight you in my heart or in my mind
I love you and yet I know you don't deserve me
So until the tides wash your footprints from my soul...I will breathe easy knowing that one day this too shall pass...

Experience

You were an experience I wanted to force to last a lifetime
Wow…you were merely an experience
I've been holding onto memories of you replaying them in my mind like my favorite movie
I memorized the lines of us in fear of forgetting what once was
Every lingering smile, every unnecessary phone call, every excuse to see me…I clung to it all as signs of hope
You were my drug and I o'ded with a DNR sign adorning my neckline
You were my breath, you were my reason to smile as I danced down memory lane, you were my lifeline
But you were merely an experience
Time after time I thought and even made small attempts to draft our last scene
The slightest chance you would entertain me…I greedily bought out the show at the idea of having you all to myself even if for only a short moment in time
Over and over and over I raked my brain trying to make sense of it all
It had to of all meant something…
You couldn't have been sent to me only to break my heart and flip my life upside down
I told you I had to have my own lane
I wanted to be something no one else was
And that which I desired I obtained
However, the package was wrapped quite differently than I had imagined
I will never forget you or our short trip to NeverLand
Note to Self: IT'S TIME TO MOVE ON
Because you were merely just an experience…

Section Two:

Excavation

The Process of Change

Thoughts running through my mind like an Olympic track meet;
positive, negative, uplifting, depressing...
all in attempts to cross the finish line first,
the prize being the opportunity to occupy space in my mind that will then affect
my mood, day, energy, presence, life...
To control my thoughts is a reality that conflicts with my own personal perception
of tasks that can be mastered
Hope, for a brighter tomorrow
Faith, that this too shall pass
Love, myself and others
Peace, of mind
A silver bracelet around my wrist that holds so much power but yet is neglected
and overlooked
The story of my life...
If others overlook and neglect me why should I not do the same?
How much weight and value could I possibly hold if no one else
sees it
nurtures it
believes in it?
Until one day on this journey through the process of change, I asked myself,
Who are these people I desire to inspire,
that I feel pulled to please,
whose yes and no hold more truth than my own?
Why do they deserve the honor
the glory
the power...more than I?
But why is irrelevant because it is
Or better yet, it was...
Taking my rightful place on the throne
No longer a puppet that is compelled to react over an action that is not my own
A shift is coming...
Lost as the words travel through my canals and out into the wind
The shift is upon me...upon us
My shift is a curve carved in my predestined path...

Rabbit Hole

What am I doing?
Who am I?
The day begins and ends like clockwork,
    a habitual routine that requires little thought as if I've been programmed
Feelings arise,
    become too much or overwhelming,
        and without effort I shut down and push forward with the next task at hand
A desire within my soul to do and be more that's quickly pushed out of the way
    making room for the next task to be completed
Years of running and hiding from me
    in fear of the repercussions that are sure to follow by breaking the mold
Trapped in a self-made cage where only I hold the key
    the key is buried under layers of
        self-doubt
            memories from the past that recreate themselves
                in the unfolding of today
Searching without looking
    looking past what I see in the mirror and into the very being of me

Suit Up

Gasping for air
    Losing my breath
    Panic setting in
    Next fear
Worried about making it
    Survival of the fittest
    Fighting for my life
        But tired of fighting...

What am I fighting for, another battle to conquer?

But I am a warrior, right?
    I've made it this far...
    I've come too far to quit now

I AM A SURVIVOR

I was uniquely designed to overcome and stand tall
Ready and waiting for my next battle
On this battlefield, I call LIFE

Thoughts Afloat

Thoughts afloat...
Drifting in and out of consciousness
Today, yesterday, then, when, etc.
Memories, fantasies, could be, and what if...
If only, maybe, and once upon a time
Smiling, laughter, heartache, pain...loss of breath
Intention, commitment, broken promises, hopes shattered
Pieces everywhere in the past, present, and future
Journey, exploration, a maze of discovery
To discover what and whom?
What is real?
What is fake?
Or is it just my imagination...running away with me?
Taste, touch, feel, see...
Belief in fairytales and happily ever afters
Nightmares, sleepwalking, illusions, and dreams
Eyes wide open without having the ability to see
Walking zombie...caught in a trance
Sunshine and storms...blessings and curses
The power of the tongue creates life and death
But what does it mean to live...truly live?
And what does it mean to be dead?
Dead in the physical sense or dead as in a human being walking around immune to the human touch and delicacies of life?
Life...a plan, a goal, or an exploration of one's self
A road map to internal bliss?
Or a scripted mini-series?
Choice, decision, erase, pause...
Director or Actor?
Creator or Receiver?
Is life dealt or is life a quest?
A quest to find, sculpt, and manifest intuitive waterfalls of desire, passion, and that which sets one's soul on fire?
Thoughts afloat...

Questions

To wonder why and then see the answer unfold itself at a later date in time
To be stuck in a feeling in the present moment and remember when the cure to a feeling
    Was to somehow..someway...
    Escape reality and hide in numbness
Pain is real, it's
    uncomfortable
        to sum it up into one word.
But yet pain holds a purpose
    a transitional movement,
        to shed the layers from what once was to what is now.
Drowning in misery, to avoid the journey of the unknown.

What is faith really?
Who is God really?
What is love really?

Is there such a thing as unconditional love?

Judgment dictating reaction and distribution of love...
Lost in a fantasy of what not to be...
Resentment
    Fear
        Anger
            Psychoanalysis
        Acceptance
    Love or Lack of
Judgment
The puppeteers of my life...

How?
    How to change?
    How to let go?
    How to maintain the desire of wanting something more?

God...
Who is he?
Who is she?
Who are they?
The plethora of concepts of a higher power...

What is right and what is wrong?
Where do you find the answers to the unknown in a know-all society?

Then culture
Our culture...
My culture...
Who says what culture belongs to whom?
You or me?

Judgment in a know-all society

What is the next step when you've been ousted from what is considered to be your own?
Lost with no direction with everyone around attempting to lead you in their direction, a direction that doesn't at all embody you

A society with all the answers except the one I'm seeking...

A key question in terms of religion...
On one hand, you're directed to seek God's will
And all is done in accordance with God's will and not your own.
With an unspoken promise that a life led in your own will,
Will in turn lead to your demise.
But on the other hand, it's said to
Ask and it shall be given
Knock and the door shall be opened
Trust and speak your desires into existence
How can the same God fulfill both when they differ so drastically?

Lost
    Seeking answers
    Unable to find the answers

How to find "my truth" when "the truth" is everywhere?

Where to turn to seek refuge in the middle of a battle zone?

Lost in thought
Lost in my head
Lost on my journey

But grateful for being given a starting point...

Battleground

Caught in the mist
Blinded by the fog
Refusing to get up
Tormented by the past
Petrified by failure
Fear has been my master
How do I separate what was in order to discover what can become
My work has become futile as I've become frozen in time
The soft green grass cradles me as I lay paralyzed watching the clouds etched with scenes from my life pass by in the crystal blue sky
Hope slowly running out like sand in an hourglass
As the last morsels fall I shatter the glass as I rise
Rise up to all that has kept me captive
Rise up to the redundancy of self-defeat
No game plan, no road map, not even an idea of how
Running on a desire to do and be more
Decision made to fight and conquer...

Breathe

Drowning in self-pity
Choking on misery
Tangled in why not
Enthralled by broken promises
Swallowed by emotion
The walls around me getting taller
The air around me getting thinner
My vision clouded by this sad story I read over and over
Defeated by my memories
Grasping for a moment in time
Dragged by my feet through the dirt of my past
Gasping for truth as I breathe in lies
Feelings bury me as I search for a numbing aid
Trials and tribulations knock me down further and further as I forget my purpose
Wiping the dust off my identity
His quote rings through the drums of my ears as I lay asleep through my awakening
The last words beat through my core knocking like the bass in my favorite tune
"Whatever you do you must keep moving forward..."

Still, I Rise

They whisper
They look
They judge
But they don't hear my cries
But they don't feel my pain
But they don't know my story
They whisper
They look
They judge
Questions swirling and being answered by those who know not
I've been convicted of a crime without first being tried
The Judge not God but my fellow peers, co-workers, friends, and family
They whisper
They look
They judge
Night after night I prayed to God asking him to forgive me of my sins
Night after night I prayed to God asking him to take away the love I have for a man who is not mine
Night after night I prayed to God asking him not to take the pain away but help me get through it
They whisper
They look
They judge
What they don't know is I hear the whispers, because I hear them in my head condemning me for my actions
What they don't know is at times I can barely look at myself in the mirror as I am filled with shame and guilt for my actions
What they don't know is I am a far more critical and harsher judge than they could ever imagine to be

They whisper
They look
They judge
I made a choice to look past right and wrong and get swept away in Never Land,
Happily Ever After, and the possibility of what if
And in my choices, I was left broken, defeated, and scattered in pieces
They whisper
They look
They judge
But through it all, I serve a mighty God who whispers his promises to my soul
But through it all, I serve a mighty God who tells me I am still the apple of his eye
But through it all, I serve a mighty God who tells me he is the only one who can
judge me
So although they whisper, look, and judge...Still, I Rise

Section Three:

Unravel

Maze

Thoughts tangled in Charlotte's Web
Mixed emotions broken down like a bag, carefully rolled up and smoked away
Trying desperately to escape,
  Running in circles only chasing my tail
Playing hide and seek with my destiny
Chasing painted images of a life not created for me
Killing myself slowly trying to fill a void with unmeasurable entities
Looking for myself in a room full of copycats
Sinking in a ship with no leak in an ocean with no water in dire need to find land to feel comfortable, when I was purposely put in this ship to go through this depth of discomfort
Lack of ambition,
  Terrified of success
Accustomed to failure but determined to prove the statistics inaccurate
Looking forward but facing backward
Ready to conquer the world but unable to find me in this maze of right and wrong turns
Lounging on cloud nine, with dirt still in my mouth from my last encounter with rock bottom
Hearing my calling for something better but listening to my present packaged tape recording telling me I'll never amount to anything more than what I dreamed of when I was sleepwalking and heard myself say no but yet experienced the opposite
Fighting for my life on a battlefield of desire to not feel
Failed attempts to erase the chalkboard filled with an intricate diagram of my life events that are only drafted and written as scripts for TV shows and movies

Blurry Vision

Struggling as I try to recapture moments, relive experiences, find the words to describe events, retrace steps taken, and gather the artifacts of my past
But yet my past is what has held me hostage for all these years
Refurbished accounts of past hurt, pain, and sorrow have built the bars to this prison I don't dare escape in fear of adding another bar
So I stay put in my prison cell of pain, self-defeat, and hopelessness because I know what to expect
At times I see the light shine and the reflection shows the way to the key that will unlock the door, but as I reach for the key, the play button is pushed and scenes from my past distort my vision of something different than that which I've become accustomed to...

Traffic Jam

Questions unanswered
Words unspoken
Feelings kept secret
A life unlived
Held back by self
Wanting but not reaching
Thinking but not knowing
Fear
Is it them or is it me?
Wanting so much to be different but trying so hard to be everyone but me...
Locked in emotions and feelings
Trying to find the key to be me, but not looking
An internal battle with my mind,
                                my heart,
                                    and my soul
Opportunities slipping past me
   Hiding
      How do I accept myself?
Thinking about how someone else would react to a situation before I react
Thinking about what I do before I do it just because of what
                                                                he/she may
                                                                    think/say
                                                                        after/while
I'm doing what I'm doing
It's like starting at the bottom of a ladder on a slide at a pool,
I climb up and down the ladder
but never make it into the water
   scared of what might happen
      because I just don't know...

Poof

Opening scars that took years to heal
Searching for myself while examining myself
Memories haunt me like nightmares, although I'm still awake
Eyes wide open
scared
what might be revealed if they shut for just a second?
Contemplating the
what ifs...
could be...
and should have
instead of maintaining acceptance of what is
Soaring in the sky observing the possibilities of a life worth living
Strategically setting myself up for failure by taking a left when the sign points to the right
Moving down yet my placement is at the top
Trigger finger happy shooting blanks at my destiny...

Hope

Feeling like every step I take despite my strategic calculations puts me on a landmine
Trying so hard to do right and be right yet in the end someone is always left disappointed, hurt, angry, or upset
Trying to configure the maze in front of me where every move I make leaves me backed into a corner
Praying but hearing nothing
Reaching out for the light but suffocating in the darkness
Ask and it shall be given
Knock and the door shall be opened
Am I mute?
Although my hands are bruised and my knuckles are worn from knocking, I'm still waiting for the door to be opened...
God knows my weaknesses, I am not ashamed to admit them but yet when I cry out for strength, I feel weak in the knees
I cry out and think my tears are nearing E, but yet the realness of the struggle maintains without halt
Tension building and throbbing in my back, neck, and head...asking for reprieve but yet the tension continues to build
PLEASE...I scream...as I feel myself sinking
Faith is the ground I aspire to stand on, yet the floor is crumbling as I scramble to hold together the pieces
I just want to do and be right, but I feel like without my knowing I was cast in Mission Impossible...
My white flag is soaring high but yet no mercy is given...
I remember as a child being under the plastic bin, I screamed, I banged, I tried with all my might to escape and then slowly as I felt my breathing shorten and my eyes get heavy...suddenly the bin was lifted and I was free
Now as an adult, without the literal bin, I feel those same feelings...the last thing I have in my pocket is a piece of hope and with that, I lay it out in front of me and am going to hope the bin of life is lifted before I take my last breath

Quicksand

Buried under feelings and suffocating from anxiety
A tug of war battle between my mind and my heart
Questioning my self-worth and doubting my strength
Blinded by flashbacks of my past; petrified to repeat history
Determined to do and be different but paralyzed by the thought of what if
Fighting for the life inside me but barely missing punches thrown by my own selfish desires
In the room with the answer but unable or maybe unwilling to reach for the light switch that will illuminate the truth...

Somewhere Over the Rainbow

Digging through the dirt of my past
trying to uncover the reasoning as to why it's all unfolded as it has
Holding a flashlight as I wander through the darkness of my mind
running into locked boxes that I sometimes sit on to keep shut
Questioning events that I see through my quest into finding myself
wondering if these events that I see are real
or
just a figment of my imagination
Were they created by this child I see alone in a room praying to God to take her in her sleep to escape the wonderland that is her reality
or
Are they real events that she has tried to seal with
broken promises
multiple partners
and freedom rolled up in a Swisher Sweet
As salty raindrops fall from her eyes slowly forming a puddle at her feet
walking away from these events
she leaves a trail of footprints leaving markings of her pain across her soul
Now back to the present moment questioning a power greater than myself
Yelling
Screaming
Cursing
Asking
WHY?!?!
Why me?
Why must I endure these stormy days where I see no rainbow
only fog hiding the reasoning behind this all...

Cyclone

A whirlwind of thoughts, feelings, and past events surround me; so fragile yet unbreakable
Unable to grasp what has unfolded before me
Frozen in a dimension unfamiliar to my sense of sight
Several reminders are needed when it comes time to breathe
A mere spectator as I watch from a distance the Jenga pieces of my life come crashing down
Blinking repeatedly to hopefully determine whether what I see and feel is real or a dream
Falling from Sears Tower, waiting to hit the pavement but yet somehow angels sent from my higher power catch me before I make contact with my final resting place...

Blah

Sadness consuming me
Trying to find the valve to turn it off
Bathing in why not, confused by what is
Empty...
Acceptance, a mere word with a hollow definition
Nauseous...
Full of you
Attempts to purge, but unwilling to let you go
Round and round like a merry go round
Just as I hear the last note and prepare to get off
My mind pushes replay and I find a new memory to get lost in
Ready to turn the next page and start a new chapter
But...
I can't find the period...

All I Know

All I know is what I know and what I've seen
Memories take me back, visiting different times and moments
Seeing shit I spent years trying to forget...
Would you really like to take a trip through my mind?
Thinking how I think
   feeling what I feel...
You have questions, you want to know why I do what I do...
Shit, you try to figure it out and see what you come up with
Let me know if you find something while you're in there
They say to forgive and forget...
What if I need a third option?
   I can't forgive...
   I won't forget...
   And I'm tired of trying...
So...what's next?

The End

Meticulously drawing a map to the end
An end with only one casualty
The intent only to breathe and break free longer than a split moment in time
The question is how
How to not break three hearts
Do I choose me or do I continue to live for others
Desperately trying to rewrite my story but all I have before me are ripped-up pages and a pile of shredded eraser
Begging for reprieve but I continue to sink
My last ounce of hope was washed away along the shore of the sea of my mind
If you see me, if you hear me…save me from me…save me from this life which has become nothing but remixed episodes of headache…heartbreak and pain
No victim in me, I know it is I who has caused and written this sad story…which too is the reason why I'm on the verge of, The End…

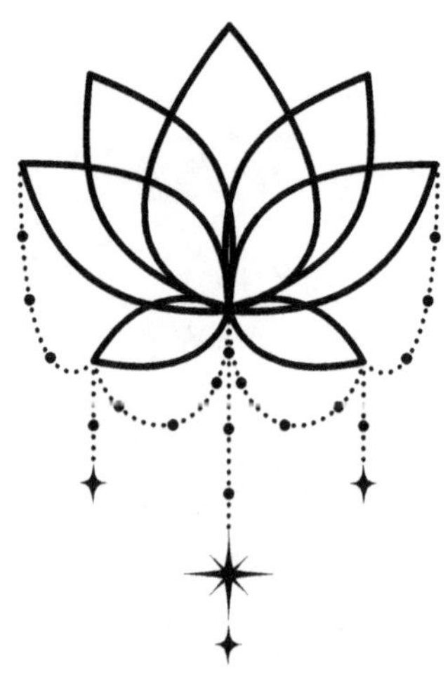

Section Four:

Lotus Flower

Reply

Who is this "her" that they speak of?
When all that is me is in alignment I see fragments of "her" through my reflection in the looking glass
This "her" whose jewels sparkle effortlessly in the very fibers that collaborate in the formation of "her"
This inferno that is spoke of resonates through the core of "her"
Finding purpose in the pool of tears that drove "her" to become "her"
When shattered pieces of "her" lay on the ground, instead of being swept up and thrown away...through the power of the most high they were instead used to cultivate the "her" she was always destined to be
Who is the "her" that they speak of?
This "her" is me...

Love

What is love, a poem written once upon a time from a mere child's perspective
Searching for love
Searching for validation
Searching for acceptance
Hoping to find it in him, in it, in this, or even in that
Needing to find it, so I can become content with me
All of my inner fill in the blanks being scribbled in with temporary vices
Destroying the pieces of me trying to create a superficial feeling of happiness
You complete me, you define me, you control me...
Looking for love in all the wrong places, vitally important and frequently heard words falling on deaf ears
Desperately searching for him to rescue me...until now
Now, I want to rediscover what love is
A love for me
A life for me
A love that is not fueled by him, it, this, or even that
I am ready for love

I Don't Need A Man

I don't need a man to love me in order to feel loved
I don't need a man to want to have sex with me in order to feel sexy
I don't need a man to desire me in order to feel beautiful
I don't need a man to sell me dreams in order to know my worth
I don't need a man to touch me to feel alive
I don't need a man to look at me to feel validated
I don't need a man to define me in order to know who I am
I don't need a man to spend time with me in order to feel special
Lessons learned...these things I now know

I Want Something More

I want something more
I blinked and saw life in a new light
As I inhaled and exhaled I felt the beat of my heart
As I sat I felt the weight of my body against my legs and the cushion of the couch gently holding up my back
I want something more
Victim? No
Survivor? Yes
But now what?
Have I gone through all that I've been through to say that I've been through something or have I gone through everything I've been through to leave my mark on this Earth?
I want something more
Life is to be lived...I've heard it and I've felt it...but now I'm ready to experience it...
Life is filled with choices, decisions, and options...each choice and decision creates a road map to my destiny. But I am the conductor...I am the director, I am the puppeteer, I am the author
The blame can no longer be passed like a game of hot potato
I'll take the L as a lesson learned and motivation to do and be better...
I want something more

Eyes Wide Open

For many years I unsuccessfully attempted to please others and make others proud of me
Always looking for that good job, pat on the back, or smile from another
Losing myself trying to live a life not created for me
But in the midst of the madness, I lied to myself and others so much that I became twisted and tangled in the false reality created by none other than me
I've realized I truly am the creator of my destiny and all that my life has been and currently is, is the result of my own penmanship
For many years I pointed my fingers at others as the cause for my heartache and pain, yet I've come to realize the culprit is the woman I see as I gaze into the mirror
Accountability is key in piecing together the authentic me
Lost and confused is a place I choose to find gratitude in just for today...

Truth

It's so easy to point the finger and blame another for our heartache, pain, and misery
Yet quite difficult to take a long look in the mirror and see ourselves and the parts we play in our heartache, pain, and misery
The layers of experiences, trials, and tribulations that shape and mold how and why we do what we do
Victimization creates pathways to the formation of culprits in future experiences, trials, and tribulations
Why is it that the answers, solutions, and exit strategies for someone else are highlighted, underlined, and shown in neon lights but when it comes to our lives we are blind to the truth?
"I want the truth..."
"...you can't handle the truth"
What I once thought was just a classic quote from a classic movie became an atomic bomb to my fantasy world
To seek the truth is one thing, to handle the truth is undoubtedly another
What do we do when what we want isn't in alignment with what is?
We shift, manipulate, force, control, maneuver, push, and pull trying to get the numbers to add up and the pieces to fit accordingly
And then once it's all said and done we point our finger outward in hopes of finding something or someone guilty of the heartache, pain, and misery that has left us speechless, lifeless, and standing in a puddle of tears
However, the perpetrator of these heinous crimes is the one whose eyes we refuse to meet when we look into that glass reflection...

Knock Knock

Knock knock
Who's there?
Me...
Me who?
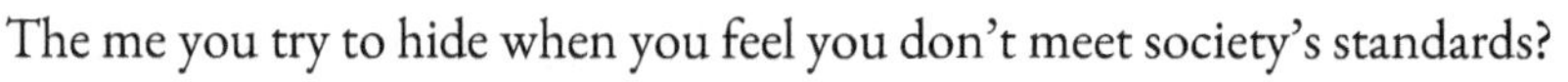
The me you try to hide when you feel you don't meet society's standards?
The me who got teased as a child and whom you've spent years trying to bury?
The me who is scared of not being accepted?
The me who is terrified of not being beautiful or desired?
The me whom you choose to overlook and ignore in hopes of finding validation through the eyes of the world?
Hello, me...
Nice to meet you

Shift

I have wanted so badly, so deeply, to find a man to fill in the blanks in my life. I believed for many years that a man would be the solution to my equation of life. My heart yearned for the, "I love you" that reached beyond the drums of my ears into the vibrations of my heartbeat.

In my mind, a man would be the cure for all my pain and suffering. I realize now that it is I who holds the keys to my happiness and freedom. It is I who holds the power and control over my here and now.

I became lost looking for the man who held the answers to my questions. I knew unconditional love from a man would validate who I am and make all that I've been through worth going through.

However, years have been wasted looking for him instead of discovering me. And now as I look around at the fruits of my labor, I see the products of a hurt, confused, lonely little girl.

I pointed my finger time and time again placing blame on unqualified men I gave myself to in hopes of righting wrongs and proving I could be everything they wanted me to be.

Falling short has left me scarred and bruised trying to customize my being to the unrealistic expectations I created in hopes of being chosen.

However, in the end, I refuse to be tainted with a bitter residue. I instead choose to love love and look into my future with wide, bright eyes knowing that whatever is meant for me never misses me and whatever misses me was never meant for me...

Thanks & Blessings

Flipping through the pages of my memory bank I see what was through a different lens
Initially, I allowed my mind to create witty comebacks and witty one-liners that would roll off my tongue sweet and innocent but leave an imprint that was bitter and stung once consumed
I questioned why the men I loved the hardest couldn't grasp what it was I wanted, needed and desired
I picked myself apart; dissecting, analyzing, and questioning what made my heart beat, brought a smile to my face, and made me feel loved because it wasn't what was brought to the table by those whom I loved the hardest
Like a shooting star through the sky, I was filled with joy and gratitude
Their leaving was a disguised blessing from God...
Their leaving has made room for "him"
The sleepless nights, the drenched pillowcases, the holes in my heart, the intentional breathing to keep that same heart beating...all held divine purpose
The dissecting, analyzing, and questioning were not done in vain... they exposed and solidified what it was I wanted, needed, and desired
And with all due respect, none of those men I loved the hardest were "him"
The him that will pursue me, the him that will love every inch, piece, and fragment of me, the him that will not himself fill...but help me find the filling to the holes in my heart, the him that will show me instead of tell me that he has me, the him who effortlessly completes me and I complete him...
Today I see what's on the other side of you letting me go...
Thanks & Blessings

Hello...Goodbye

Hello, Jealousy mixed with a shot of Envy...
So we meet again...
I often don't know you've entered the room until I feel your breath on the back of my neck
As I turn my head to see who is there
You creep through my pores and it is you I see when I blink and open my eyes
You become a filter, a perspective, a beautifully disguised lie I struggle to grasp the truth of
You encapsulate me and based on our level of familiarity...I don't know you've left me until I take the time to become grounded, centered, and uncover another piece of the authentic me
As hard as it is to say this, I think it's time for us to see other people
I want to see people from the inside out, no longer comparing and contrasting brewing toxic batches of self-abuse, self-loathing, self-deception, self-pity, and self-immolation
It's time to break free, spread my wings, and fly
Goodbye and thank you for the time we've spent as I'm beginning to learn that lessons learned are never time misspent...

Section Five:

Blossom

Finding Purpose In My Pain

Pain has been my teacher
Pain has been my confidant
Pain has been my mirror
Pain has been my tool
I have run from pain while diving into the pain
I have held pain and I have caused pain
I thought the pain was destroying me and instead it was uncovering me
I thought the pain was breaking me and instead it was molding me
I thought the pain I felt was a punishment and instead it was a testament
I thought the pain was suffocating me and instead it was teaching me how to breathe with purpose
I thought the pain was killing me and instead it was birthing me
I thought the pain would end me and it did...but only to free me

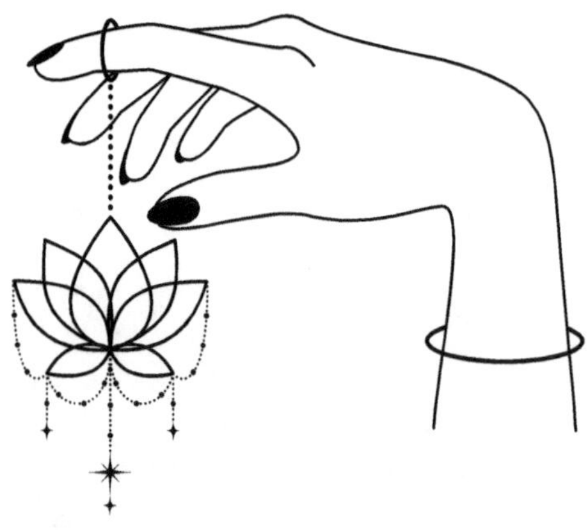

www.ingramcontent.com/pod-product-compliance
Lightning Source LLC
LaVergne TN
LVHW010500160826
845677LV00012B/2577

* 9 7 9 8 9 8 7 9 8 7 9 3 3 *